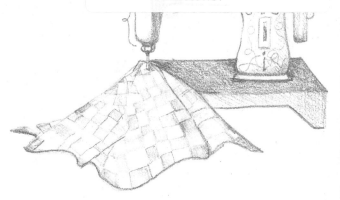

A QUILTER'S Notebook

Design and illustrations by Cheryl A. Benner

Quotations reprinted with permission from: Nancy Crow in
Home Quilt Show magazine, Big Sandy, Texas; Sherrie Jaqua
in *Quilting Today,* (#13) June/July 1989, pg. 50 and (#15)
Oct./Nov. 1989, pg. 23; Rosalee Courtney and D.J. Parkhill
in *Quilting Today,* (#15), pg. 17; Judy B. Dales in *Quilting
International;* Gale Research Company; Susan Lawson in
Amish Patchwork, Dover Publications, Inc.; Marguerite Ickis
in *The Standard Book of Quilt Making and Collecting,*
©1949, Dover Publications, Inc.; Jean Ray Laury and Lys
Ann Shore in *Quilter's Newsletter Magazine;* Carter Houck
for *Patchwork Quilts Magazine; Erica Wilson's Quilts
of America,* ©1979, Oxmoor House; Ami Simms in
American Quilter; Kathryne Hall Travis in the *South-
west Review,* ©1930; *Capper's Weekly;* Rachel T.
Pellman and Joanne Ranck in *Quilts Among the Plain
People* ©1981, Good Books; Judy Schroeder Tomlonson
in *Mennonite Quilts and Pieces,* ©1985, Good Books.

"The most difficult part about making a quilt is choosing the right colors and prints for your fabrics."

"Like songs we hear on the radio that conjure strong memories of a particular time and place, quilts have a way of reminding us."

"When my father had his heart attack, he was told not to do any manual labor, so he bought a sewing machine and he went to work and appliqued quilt tops."

"Quilting is so relaxing, especially when there is a snowstorm outside."

"I have been renewing my family history memories—not with pen and paper but with needle and thread."

"Quilting was a creative expression that we didn't have elsewhere. At least that is true for those of us who are of Amish background."

"For some the process is just as much fun as the product; we quilt-a-holics enjoy every time consuming stitch."

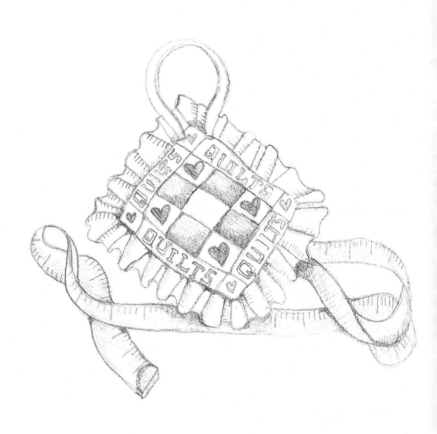

"Because quilters share a set of skills and an appreciation of textiles, we have a way to leap over the social, cultural, or historical barriers that might otherwise separate us."

"Now they call it a quilting bee, but back then we just called it a party."

"What would you rather have written on your tombstone, 'She was a great housekeeper,' or 'Here lies a wonderful quilter who left behind many beautiful quilts to keep her family warm for generations'? I know what I'd choose."

"You can't always change things. Sometimes you don't have no control over the way things go. Hail ruins the crops or fire burns you out. And then you're just given so much work within a life and you have to do the best you can with what you've got. That's what piecing is."

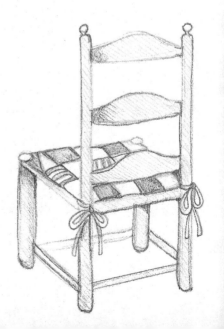

"Quilting builds on itself—if you cut your pieces accurately in the beginning, you're more likely to come out with something beautiful in the end."

"So they are all there in that quilt, my hopes and fears, my joys and sorrows, my loves and hates. I tremble sometimes when I remember what that quilt knows about me."

"When I'm not creating I'm not happy. And I'm a nicer person to live with when allowed time to create. Quilting keeps me sane."

"It is easy to create for approval, but usually not as satisfying."

"When a girl was thinkin' on marryin', and we all done a lot of that, she had to start thinkin' on gettin' her quilts pieced."

One Mennonite woman remembers quilting parties where newspapers would be spread on the finished quilt and then the family cat would be put in the middle. The unmarried nieces called to the cat and whoever it ran to was "the next one married."

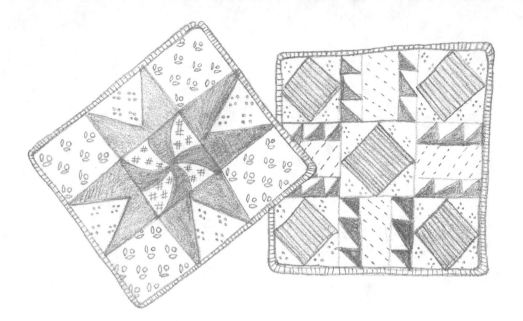

"Within the world of quiltmaking there is so much possibility for play—especially visual play, trying endless variations of arrangements, colors, patterns without any preconceived notions as to the results."

"Those individuals who pursue their passions, who work at what they most enjoy, are just a tad suspect."

In Fall of 1935, the Sears Roebuck catalog offered these bargains: eight piecing templates for 9¢; twenty-one quilting patterns for 23¢; one pound of quilting fabric (enough for an average-size quilt top) costing 21¢; and a quilting frame for $2.95!

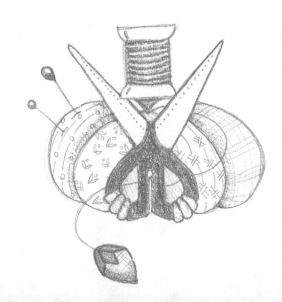

"My mother really liked color, and you could especially see that in the quilts she made. I think, because the times could be so hard, the colors brightened up her world."

"My husband cut the patches for all the quilts I made for my grandchildren."

"Mother used what she had, feed sacks. At that time you just didn't go out and buy new material."

"Quilters are tactile artists. Quilters are observant people."

"Years ago the mothers didn't work away like they do these days so they had time to quilt—and the children used to play underneath the quilt."

"Take a chance or two. Quilts are much more interesting if people try to do something different with color and design."

"A quilt is a reminder of our ancestors who, because of their faith in God's guidance, had courage to strike out for new lands without knowing what awaited them."

"When you make a quilt you really achieve something. A quilt is something which lasts a long, long time."

"My mother's flower gardens provided color lessons I'll never forget."

"Grandmother was very much of a quilt lady. Every time we visited her, she'd have another new quilt top ready."

"I learned to sew by sewing four-patches by hand before I went to school."

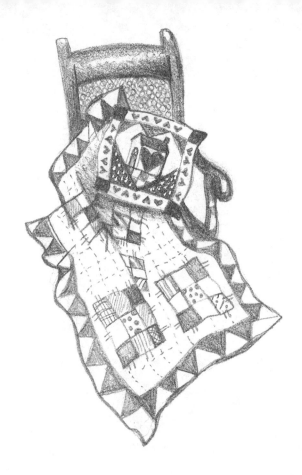

"Years ago, the idea of quilting was to use up your old material. It was our parents being frugal—it was their way of life."

"The artistic part of it is that there are always new patterns to try and new things to think about. You've always got some new idea in your head."

"Quilting isn't difficult—it just takes a lot of patience."

"I don't know how we do it, but we quilt about as fast as we talk."

"My first quilt was a four-patch sewn together by hand. My mom used to say, 'You have to make a patch before you go out to play.'"

"I still remember a silk quilt we had that my grandmother made. I'm partly responsible for the fact that it's no longer around. My friends and I used to slide down the stairs on it."

"Relying on my feelings and instincts allows a lot of myself to become a part of the quilt."

"... now this here quiltin', well I jes' went out in the yard and got some leaves off the rosebush and laid 'em down and drawed 'round them, and made my own quiltin' pattern."

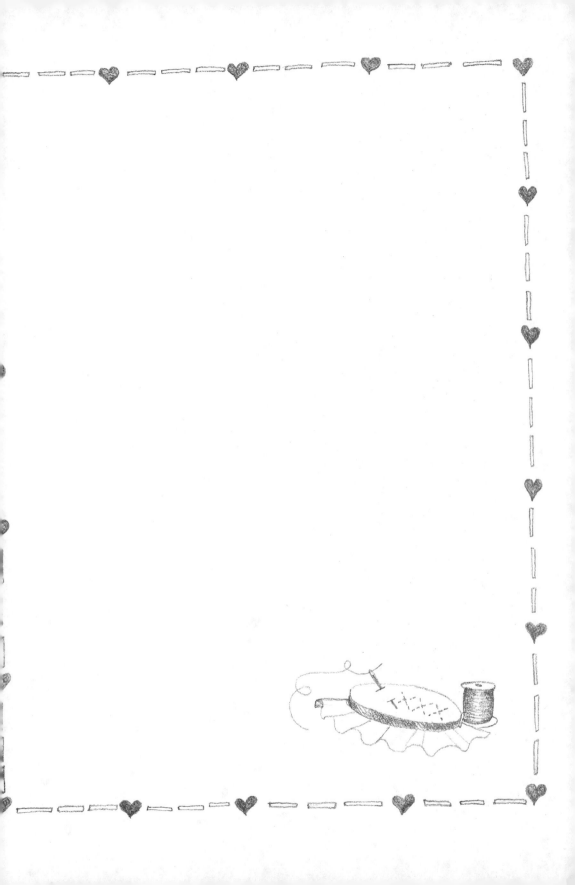

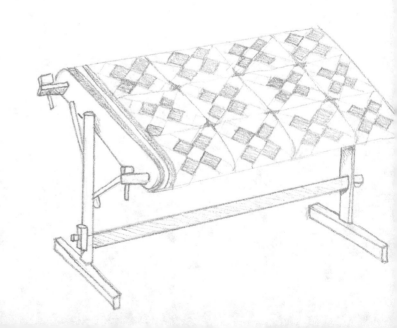

"When Lizzie and I were younger, we'd put a quilt in on a Monday and try to have it done till the next Sunday."

"A quilt has to grow as it is made; graphing it out ahead of time seems to close the door to flexibility and improvement."

The oldest surviving example of patchwork is a colored gazelle on the canopy of an Egyptian queen in the year 980 B.C.—at the time of King Solomon.

"We used what we had on hand in those days and then, because we needed orchid and yellow, we dyed feed sacks to get those."

"Quilting was a winter activity for my Nebraska grand-mother. Piecing was done during the summer in spare moments between chores, gardening and canning and, often, field work for the same women."

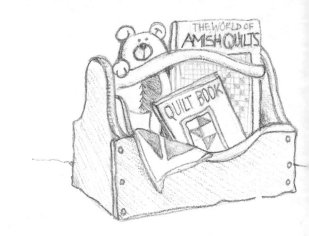

"Color is the key ingredient to the life one feels when viewing an Amish quilt."

"It was a tradition earlier to make an 'error' in each quilt because, it was pointed out, 'only God is perfect.' These errors were to demonstrate your humility."

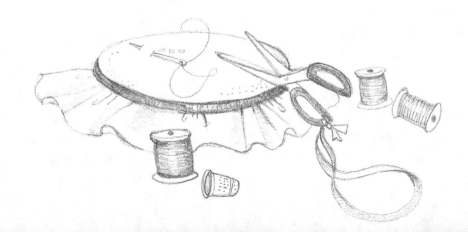

"My old man's ma was a hand at makin' quilts. She made one with over six thousand pieces in hit, but the young ones done tore hit up."

"Why do I keep coming to quilt here at church? You know, at the age of 82 or 83, it is a way to feel useful, and I love the fellowship."